Write Your Memoir
One Story at a Time

Write Your Memoir

One Story at a Time

Susie H. Baxter

ISBN 978-0-9980828-0-6
Available from Amazon.com and other retail outlets

To my grandmother,
whose loss made me recognize
the importance of asking questions
before it's too late

Acknowledgements

My sincere thanks to

Dr. Hilda K. Ross for her encouragement to write about my rural roots when I took the classes she offered at the Millhopper Library and for inviting me to teach her course when she moved from Gainesville.

Audrey Frank and other members of the Millhopper Library staff for their support in the early days—and to Santa Fe College for providing another venue.

Joan Carter, Ann-Marie Magné, Wendy Thornton, Kaye Linden, and Bonnie Ogle for critiquing story after story, as well as this manual. Their questions and suggestions have been invaluable.

Jeanne Field, my editor, for identifying dozens of typos I overlooked. Unfortunately, when I correct one error, I tend to introduce another, so any mistakes readers find are my fault entirely.

Gil Baxter, who must wish that cooking held as much interest for me as writing.

Finally, to those who have passed through courses I've taught, who have shown me, time and time again, that everyone has fascinating stories to tell.

Contents

Preface

This manual evolved from a five-week course I teach on writing memoir. It's packed with writing prompts, exercises, questionnaires, and assignments to help prod your memory. You could read cover to cover within an hour or two. But don't. Take your time. Take five weeks if needed. Complete the exercises and assignments as you go. If you do, you'll be well into your memoir before you reach the last page.

> "Writing memoir is a way to figure out who you used to be and how you got to be who you are."
> — Abigail Thomas

Whether you are writing to discover yourself, leave a legacy for your descendants, or publish a best seller, my goal is to help you get started and provide guidance as you dig deeper.

I also encourage you to sign up for a course in memoir writing and join a writers group. You will glean ideas from fellow writers and benefit from their feedback.

Now, let's leap into your life!

1

One Story, Then Another

Each of us has unique experiences and ideas that might entertain and benefit others, but unless we record them, they're likely to die with us. Consider the quote at right, often attributed to Alex Haley, the author of *Roots*.

> *"When a person dies, a small library burns."*
> — Alex Haley

You are a repository of experiences. Which of your memories might interest others?

Perhaps you recognize that writing about your life is important, but you've hesitated. Why did you put it off? What was the excuse, up to now, legitimate or not?

- I was too busy.
- I didn't know where to begin.
- The task was too daunting—so many years to cover.
- Who would be interested in reading about me? I'm not famous.
- I didn't want to brag or air dirty laundry.

- I didn't want to make embarrassing mistakes.
- I'm not a writer.
- I'm not sure how to structure it and how much to cover.
- I can't remember portions of my life.

Exercise 1.1 — I can't remember

Write a sentence or paragraph about what you cannot remember very well—but wish you could.

As we write, we recall more and more. And with memoir, we don't have to recall everything at once, or everything period, since we are not writing about our entire lives—not yet, anyway.

AUTOBIOGRAPHY VERSUS MEMOIR

Autobiography and memoir are written from the first-person point of view. The differences between the two are narrowing, but traditionally an autobiography covers a person's entire life, whereas a memoir concentrates on a portion or one aspect of a person's life, such as one's passion.

Writing about every year you've lived would probably feel overwhelming. So, zero in on one portion of your life and work to complete that first. The task will be less daunting.

A person writes only one autobiography but may write several memoirs. Frank McCourt, for example, wrote three: *Angela's Ashes* deals with his Irish childhood; *'Tis* tells of his transition from impoverished immigrant to American teacher; and *Teacher Man* describes his bumpy career in a New York City high school.

For a more detailed description of autobiography and memoir, check out the Center for Autobiographic Studies: *http://www.centerautobio.org/autobiographic-writing/*

HOW DO YOU LEARN TO WRITE MEMOIR?

By writing. And by reading other memoirs. For the next few weeks, I encourage you to put aside your novels and magazines and concentrate on reading memoirs. Although there's no right or wrong way to write a memoir, reading what others have written will provide ideas on how to structure yours. See Recommended Memoirs in the Appendix (p. 99).

Exercise 1.2 — Interesting reads

Recall three books that held your interest—books you continued to think about after you put them down. List them, and answer these questions:

Why did the books hold your interest?
Did you relate to the characters?
Were the characters humorous?
Did they remind you of people you know or have known?
Did they reveal their humanness?
Did they make mistakes? Overcome obstacles?
Did you learn from the books? If so, what?

My favorite three books (all memoir and in the coming-of-age or *Bildungsroman* category) are Frank McCourt's *Angela's Ashes*, Maya Angelou's *I Know Why the Caged Bird Sings,* and Russell Baker's *Growing Up*. Why? McCourt was able to look back on his impoverished childhood with humor and grace; he inspired me to write about my rural childhood. Angelou explored a difficult topic—rape—with honesty. And Baker, a Pulitzer Prize winner, showed how courage and hard work pays off.

WHO ARE YOU?

A few years ago, the online magazine *Smith* launched a six-word memoir project. The magazine's tagline said: "Everyone has a story. What's yours?"

Hundreds of people submitted. Some sent six words to describe their lives; others created a six-word description for a famous person. Here's a sampling:

> "Smokes, spits, scratches, wins baseball games."
> — Baseball manager Jim Leyland

> "Brought it to a boil. Often."
> — Chef Batali

> "Michigan girl became famous, then English."
> — Madonna

> "Dated tall guys. Didn't marry one."
> — Wife of Neal Rubin, *Detroit News*

"Standing up can mean sitting down."
— Rosa Parks

Think about your life—your entire life—and complete the following exercise.

Exercise 1.3 — Six-word memoir

Write your name as you would like it to appear on your tombstone, followed by the six words that best describe the qualities or values that have made you the unique person you are.

WHY DO YOU WISH TO WRITE ABOUT YOUR LIFE?
Many emerging memoirists say, "I want to write about my life for my family." That's reason enough. That was my response nearly two decades ago. I hoped my children and grand-children, raised in the city, would enjoy reading about my rural childhood. I didn't expect a larger audience, since I considered my life quite ordinary.

But fellow writers in my critique groups tell me that my life was anything but ordinary. To them, ordinary is growing up with a telephone, a television, and indoor plumbing—all unknown to me as a child. Many of us may think our lives were ordinary when, in reality, they were extraordinary.

Exercise 1.4 — Why? For whom? Message?

Write one paragraph that answers these three questions:

> *Why do I want to write about my life?*
> *For whom do I wish to write?*
> *What do I hope readers will learn from my memoir?*

While your initial intention may be to write for yourself or family members, you never know. Your story might have universal appeal.

WHERE WILL YOU START?
Actually, you've already started. Your six-word memoir could be the inspiration for your title. Your reason for writing, from Exercise 1.4 above, might be the draft for your preface. Moving forward, now, concentrate on one story at a time.

As a memoirist, you have an advantage over fiction writers. Your stories are already in your head. You know your main character inside and out, so you won't have to do as much research. While you may be tempted to begin with your birth, I suggest you begin instead with an event that's vivid in your memory. Eventually, you can go back and write about the day you were born. You may also want to connect your stories, one to the other; but for now, concentrate on stand-alone stories.

Exercise 1.5 — A place where you felt safe

Close your eyes and think back to a place where you once felt safe. Draw the layout of that place in the box below (or on a separate sheet of paper). It might be your childhood home. It could be the home of a grandparent or a good friend—even a school or church. If it's a house you draw, where did you eat? Sleep? Do you remember incidents that took place in some of the rooms, in the yard, or on the street or neighborhood that you want to write about? Jot them down. Outside, add trees, sidewalk, fences, etc.

Or, complete this exercise, showing a place you felt unsafe.

HOW LONG WILL IT TAKE?

A friend of mine completed a memoir about her career in less than a year. But she didn't do much else during that time. Most of us are still living life fully and we have families or other obligations. A year probably won't allow enough time to write, reflect, edit, and obtain feedback on a complete memoir. With that in mind, I suggest you plan to work on yours for about two years. It could take even longer. Don't rush the process, but set a goal and work diligently toward it.

That being said, if you think or know you don't have long to live and want to leave a legacy for family, write first about what's most important, and publish your stories in small volumes as you work toward covering a longer period of time.

OBTAINING FEEDBACK

In the beginning, do not share your writing with family and friends. I learned this lesson the hard way. When I took my first writing class, the instructor told us students not to share stories with family or friends because we might receive negative feedback that would stifle the creative process.

I didn't listen; I was too eager to have my sisters read stories I'd written about our childhood. I gave one sister a chapter one day and watched as she read, expecting her to laugh or nod her head in approval.

A paragraph down the page, she said, "This is wrong." After another paragraph, she repeated, "This is wrong." And at the bottom of the first page, she said, "It didn't happen this way."

Recognize that no two people, not even conjoined twins, will see events the same. For now, do not share your stories with family members.

Friends, on the other hand, are likely to say, "It's marvelous," whether it is or not. I recommend, as my first instructor did, that you refrain from sharing your stories with family or friends. You're more apt to receive positive and constructive feedback in a classroom atmosphere from strangers who don't already know the story. In Chapter 5, we'll talk more about the benefits of joining a writing group.

CHOOSING TOPICS

When I suggest an exercise or topic for you to write about, it is just that: a suggestion. If you prefer to write on a different topic, do so. And if you have time to write more than one story at a sitting, do that too. The more stories you write each day, each week, each month, the sooner you'll reach your goal.

As you write your first draft, don't be concerned about overusing the personal pronoun *I*. Forget about spelling, grammar, and punctuation. Write without stopping to edit. Just move the story from your head to the page as Stephen King says he does. Bad writing is better than no writing.

> *"Downloading what's in my head directly to the page, I write as fast as I can . . . . I write rapidly, putting down my story . . . [so] I can keep up with my original enthusiasm and at the same time outrun the self-doubt that's always waiting to settle in."*
>
> —Stephen King

A draft is a preliminary sketch. It is expected to be rough and unpolished. Remember that the word *draft* also means *a flow of air*, so let your thoughts flow freely, like a draft of air through an open window.

Exercise 1.6 — Two-page story

Write as quickly as you can about a person who has had a great impact on your life (positive or negative). You need not recall conversations verbatim, but the gist of dialogue should be as accurate as you can make it. Give the reader a sense of the year and how old you were at the time.

To each story you write, add a title, your name, and the date as shown on the sample story that begins on page 89. If using a computer, make sure you save the digital file, and I suggest you also print a copy.

Complete the Early Childhood Questionnaire, p. 65.

2

Commit to It

Life stories do not write themselves. They require a commitment of time. If you absolutely cannot devote the time to write the stories yourself, consider these alternatives:

- Purchase a ready-made book that asks questions (e.g., *My Story: A Fill-in-the-blank Autobiography*, by Alex A. Lluch), and write the answers in the book.

- Purchase transcription software such as Dragon. Dictate into it, and the words will be recorded in text format. Keep in mind, however, that such software does not distinguish between homophones (e.g., write/right).

- Hire a ghostwriter. Tell your story to a person who will write it for you. Nathan Whitaker, for example, wrote Tony Dungy's memoir, *Quiet Strength,* and Tim Tebow's *Through My Eyes.* Hiring a ghostwriter, of course, is likely to be the most expensive option.

Most of us can write the stories ourselves if we make minor changes in our lives to free up a few hours. When I began to write my memoir, I would ask myself, *Do I really need to go shopping today? Do I need to watch this television program? Should I spend the afternoon playing bridge or writing?*

We are in control of a good chunk of our time, but well-meaning friends and family can usurp our time if we allow it. It's often just a matter of choice. If finding the hours means you must give up another activity, what will it be? Is there something you have been doing out of habit but don't really enjoy? Then give that up. You are a writer now. And writers must guard their time. Make a pledge to yourself that you will begin. Then set aside the hours to write.

YOUR BEST PLACE TO WRITE

Determine where you do the best writing. Is it sitting at a desk? On the living room sofa? In a coffee shop? At a park? Determine what works best for you and stick to a routine.

> **What works for you?**
>
> A spot that's free of distractions?
> Total silence?
> Background music?

ASSEMBLE SUPPLIES

Purchase several notepads and place them, along with a pen or pencil, around your house, in your car, and in your purse or pocket, so you can jot down ideas as they come to you.

> Place notepads everywhere you work and play!

Memory can be fleeting. You may think of something today that you want to write about, but if you fail to record a few trigger words, a particular memory might never resurface.

Arrange your writing supplies and materials so everything is together when you sit down to write, whether you use a computer or pen and paper.

If you write your draft in longhand, you can type it later—although that isn't absolutely necessary.

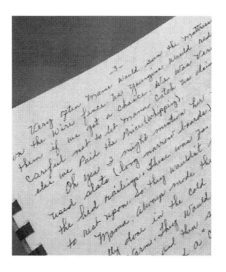

One of my cousins wrote hers in longhand, then had it printed and comb bound for her family. The handwritten memoir is so personal—a treasure to family members— mistakes and all. I loved reading it.

If you plan to use a traditional publisher, however, your work must be typed on a computer. Today's publishers expect electronic files, double-spaced manuscript with one-inch margins, and a standard font, such as Times New Roman. Also, go easy on formatting (e.g., bold, italics, tabs, fancy fonts).

ESTABLISH A FILING SYSTEM
If you use a computer, save your stories to an electronic file, print them, and/or place a backup file on a flash drive or a

cloud storage system such as Dropbox or One Drive (Microsoft). Imagine how you would feel if you failed to back up a chapter and your computer crashed. What if you lost ten chapters?

SET A SCHEDULE

Many writing teachers and coaches tell you to write every day. That's perhaps the best way to improve and reach your goal. But that doesn't work for everyone. If I sit down to write in the morning, I will still be at my computer at dinnertime. Once I get going, I don't want to stop. I must allocate certain days for writing and other days for chores and errands.

Establish a writing routine, but you know yourself, so work out your own schedule.

CONSIDER THE SCOPE OF YOUR WORK

As you read other memoirs, you'll see there are endless ways to organize your material and different places to start. One memoir might begin with childhood, another might pick up in midlife, still another might begin in old age and move forward or reflect.

Exercises in this book are meant to help you sort through your life experiences and decide where to start and how much to cover. If you already know exactly what you wish to include in your memoir, you are ahead of most, but the exercises should still be beneficial.

First, let's look back at the decades. How many decades have you lived?

Exercise 2.1 — Decades of your life

List all the decades you've lived. Leave three or four lines of space between each. Then go back and, in any order, write a sentence or short paragraph about each decade—what that decade was like for you and what, if anything, was going on in the world around you. You will likely remember some decades more clearly than others. Fill in each blank as best you can. Now ask yourself: What was my best decade? Worst decade? Label them. Then write one page about the best decade and two pages about the worst decade.

> 1940s: Played . . .
>
> 1950s: School was . . .
>
> 1960s: I was in college but not considered one of the cool hippies. I didn't smoke pot— wasn't a flower child. In fact, I already had a child of my own.
>
> 1970s – Moved to . . .

Also, devise a system for looking back at the years of your life. One way is to use index cards, one for each year that you plan to cover in your memoir. As ideas for stories come to you, jot down trigger words on the appropriate cards.

Another method is to create a memory chart (see next page) on which you list all the years on the left, with columns for miscellaneous information. Put snippets down as you think of them. Keep going back to fill in more and more blanks. This memory-chart method is the one Dr. Hilda K. Ross recommends in *Writing Your Life History: A Journal of Self-*

Discovery, an excellent resource if you plan to eventually write about your entire life.

Year	Age	Address/School/Job	Story Ideas	World Events
1944	birth	RR 4, Bradford, FL		
1945	1			War ended
1946	2			
1947	3		First memory	
1948	4		The flood	
1949	5			
1950	6	Kirby School, grade 1	1st day of school	
1951	7		Teased about teeth	
1952	8		Best friend Jean	

SHOULD YOU WRITE CHRONOLOGICALLY?

The answer is *no.* As mentioned in Chapter 1, do not begin with the day you were born—unless the story includes some unusual circumstance of major importance to your memoir (e.g., your mother passed away giving birth to you).

Write first about experiences you feel are most important to record. None of us knows how much time we have on earth. So, write first about the experiences that affected you most, or about people and events that are most important to you.

Later on, if you want to write about your birth, research the date to determine if you can connect it to some world event, giving your reader a sense of that particular time.

Use Bernard Grun's *The Timetables of History* or search the Web for information. Here's an example:

> *The White House was occupied by FDR. The U.S. was engaged in a second world war. Anne Frank was writing about the last days of her life when mine was about to begin.*

There is no right or wrong way to organize your memoir. You may have to write several stories before you decide. You could organize material according to milestones in your life, such as graduations, weddings, births, jobs, locations lived, or by subject: education, romance, rearing children, career, travel, etc. Janis Owens's memoir, for example, revolves around her southern family's recipes: *The Cracker Kitchen: A Cookbook in Celebration of Cornbread-Fed, Down-Home Family Stories and Cuisine.* Now that's a mouthful.

Since I consider myself a *cracker,* like Owens, I adore the way she "peels back the historic misconceptions connected with the word [cracker] to reveal a breed of proud, fiercely independent Americans with a deep love of their families, their country, their stories . . . ." But here I've gone off topic. Sorry!

Only after you've decided on the theme and scope of *your* memoir should you worry about organizing your stories. However, to each story you write, add a title and the date you think the event occurred. This will help later when you *do* organize your material into a coherent whole.

IDEAS IF STUMPED

If you have writer's block when you sit down to write, read through the list below for ideas.

Experiences with relatives (parents, siblings, etc.)

Toys, pets, playmates

Where you have lived—neighborhood, neighbors

Schools, teachers, classmates/friends, favorite subjects

Birthday celebrations, holidays

Illnesses, remedies, visits to doctor, surgeries

How did the Great Depression affect you or
your parents?

How did the military or the war affect you or those close
to you?

Summer vacations

Hobbies or favorite activities

TV programs and movies

Talents

Books read

Music

Failures, hopes/dreams

Religious or spiritual beliefs

Property owned

Work issues

Travel

Retirement

Children and grandchildren

Volunteer work

What do you want others to know about you?

What *don't* you want others to know?

Still having problems? Think of all the firsts you can write about . . .

your first memory
your first teacher
your first friend
your first pet
your first loose tooth
your first visit to a dentist
your first swim
your first car, boat, train, airplane ride
your first trip, trip abroad
your first kiss
your first love
your first dance
your first serious illness
your first visit with an OB/GYN or urologist
your first funeral
your first job
your first paycheck
your first traffic ticket
your first traffic accident
your first marriage
your first house
your first child

Can you think of other firsts you can add to the list?

Included in the Appendix is a list of questions (p. 81) meant to oust writer's block. Tear out the pages or photocopy them, cut the questions apart, and drop them into a large jar. Later, when you're stumped for a topic to write about, pull a surprise question from the jar. This can be fun. While it may not elicit a story that will fit within your memoir, no writing is ever wasted. It's practice.

Also, search the Web for life questions. Numerous websites (e.g., *www.mseffie.com/handouts/110personal.html*) offer thought-provoking questions like these:

> What did you think you would grow up to be?
>
> Did you? Why or why not?

> If you were starting over, would you take a different
>
> path? What would it be?

> Did you ever stand up to a bully? Did you ever bully
>
> someone?

Exercise 2.2 — Brainstorm

The standard prompt for fiction writers is "What if?" The standard prompt for memoir writers is "I remember," which can be followed by words that trigger memories. Begin with the five senses and then branch out.

I remember smelling . . .
I remember tasting . . .
I remember hearing . . .
I remember seeing . . .

I remember feeling . . .
I remember thinking . . .
I remember loving . . .
I remember hating . . .
I remember wondering . . .

Yes, keep going! Fill at least one page. Then choose one from your list, and complete as many as possible. For example:

I remember smelling chlorine in the city pool.
I remember smelling bread baking in Grandma's oven.
I remember smelling . . .

Complete the Early Schooldays Questionnaire, p. 67.

3

Memories to Pages

Actress Marilu Henner and a handful of people in the U.S. have been diagnosed with a mental condition called H-SAM, Highly Superior Autobiographical Memory. These people can recall details from almost every day of their lives.

The vast majority of us, of course, are not endowed with a perfect memory, and this is actually a good thing when it comes to writing about our past. Nobody would want to read a memoir that told about every minute of every day—no matter how famous the person. It would be encyclopedic.

Whatever the average person can recall represents what is most valuable. The memories that stick with us are the ones most charged with emotion. As might be expected, we remember goof-ups and painful events more clearly than happiness and bliss.

If our memories were fabric, of course, the fabric would be tattered, torn, and full of holes. The worn fabric might even have a few patches because someone reminded us of an event we'd almost forgotten, and their telling patched our memory.

For that reason, I think it's best to record your memories as *you* remember them before discussing experiences with those who shared them with you. Otherwise, your memory may be clouded by their version. If you ask a brother, for example, how something happened, his version will likely be different. If he insists he's right, ask him to write his version. Then, include it. Or include a disclaimer—"My brother disagrees with me, but I think . . . ." Only if the information you've recorded is proven wrong should you alter your story.

That does happen. When I wrote about my "first date," I said it occurred the summer of 1957. Note that I put quotes around *first date* because I'm sure my college-age cousin who was entertaining me, his junior-high cousin, did NOT consider it a date. My sister said she thought my first date took place later than '57. Turns out she was right. When I Googled the title and release date of the movie my cousin took me to, *The Vikings* with Kirk Douglas, I learned the film did not debut until '58.

IMPERFECT MEMORY

Everyone's memory can be questioned; one's memory is not always identical to facts or history. And even if two individuals have the same experience, they're apt to remember it differently because they don't give it the same attention or have the same perspective. We've all heard how witnesses to a traffic accident will give conflicting statements to the police, even to the color of cars involved.

My husband and I came face to face with the reality of being imperfect witnesses. Truth, we learned, is often in the eye of the beholder.

I'll tell the story in present tense—the way Frank McCourt wrote much of *Angela's Ashes*. Present tense can make it seem as if you're experiencing something for the very first time. Some believe this aids recall.

> *One morning, we're reading the newspaper and I hear arguing and cursing outside. We're new to the neighborhood. I don't know all the neighbors yet, but I'm aware that the young woman who lives across the street took out a restraining order against her former live-in boyfriend.*
>
> *I go to the front window to see what's going on. Three men are arguing with a young woman. It appears they are trying to force my neighbor into a black SUV parked in the street, motor running.*
>
> *"Something crazy is going on," I say to my husband, "I'm calling the police." As I call 911 and give my location, the woman is shoved into the SUV. The man who shoved her scoots in next to her; another guy hops into the driver's seat, and the third goes into the house.*
>
> *My husband joins me at the window long enough to give me the make and model of the SUV the 911 operator asks for, then returns to his recliner and newspaper.*
>
> *The black SUV speeds away, tires squealing, at which time I see another black SUV in the driveway. It had been obscured by the one in the street.*

The man who went inside the house comes out with a bag in his hand, gets in the second SUV, backs out of the driveway, and speeds away. I'm now convinced my neighbor has been abducted—and robbed.

Within minutes a uniformed officer knocks at our door. My husband joins me at the door to relate what happened. When I tell the officer about the three men and two SUVs, my husband disputes this, saying there was only one vehicle. The officer looks puzzled.

He goes across the street and knocks on my neighbor's front door. What does he think he's doing? I wonder. She's not there! Those men took her! The policeman didn't believe me. To my astonishment, her front door opens a few inches. The officer stands there several minutes, talking.

He walks back to our house and reports that all is well. "Your neighbor and her girlfriend went out partying last night," he says. "The girlfriend had too much to drink and decided to spend the night with your neighbor, rather than drive herself home—which was good. Unfortunately, she didn't call her husband to let him know, and his two buddies had been helping him search for her all night. The second SUV belonged to her."

In the example above, my husband and I thought we saw the same thing, but we didn't. I thought my neighbor had been hauled away. My conclusion was dead wrong. If we'd written about what we saw before the police officer clarified the situation, we would have written two different stories and both would have been wrong.

Even if people see the same thing, it can register differently, as the following exercise will demonstrate.

Exercise 3.1 — One picture, two views

Have yourself and a friend view the same magazine picture for thirty seconds. Close the magazine and each of you write a description, providing enough detail that someone who never saw the picture could visualize it. Then compare your descriptions.

OUTLINE OR PLUNGE IN?

When you're ready to write a story, should you outline or plunge in? There are no rules. If you are writing in longhand, an outline might be a good idea (less rewriting). If you wish to write about a broad topic or one that's not clear in your head, a *memory wheel* or *mind map* might help.

Exercise 3.2 — Create a memory wheel

Write "Schooldays" in the center of the page (or another topic of choice). Circle it. Then add wheel spokes on which you write words that relate to your topic. Continue to branch out, adding more spokes. Create memory wheels for four more topics (e.g., family, friends, jobs, leisure time, hobbies, entertainment, travel, world events, health, sexuality, spirituality). After completing the memory wheels, choose one and write a story about that topic in *present tense*; include information you've written on the spokes. Save the other memory wheels for later.

VOICE

Memoir is normally written in the first person, so use your own unique voice. Don't try to sound like someone you are not. In other words, write the way you talk.

Look at these two writing samples that describe the same meal:

> *My grandmother prepared a delicious dinner of crispy chicken, peas—and extremely hot muffins to which I added a pat of butter.*

> *Grandma fixed us a finger-lickin'-good supper—fried chicken, peas, and steamin' cornbread that melted the butter as I smeared it.*

What does each voice tell you?

A dictionary and thesaurus can be useful to help find the *right* word, but be careful not to overdo it, or the story will not sound authentic.

MOOD

In the previous chapter, you used all the senses to prod your memory. Also use the five senses in your writing to help set the mood.

What senses are used in this excerpt?

> *Daddy parked by the loading dock in full sun, got out of the truck, and went into Castleberry's Seed and Feed. With no breeze to speak of, the cab of the truck soon felt like an oven set for baking biscuits. A bead of sweat tickled my neck as it trickled down. The smell of cut grass drifted our way from a patch of Bahia grass a man was mowing near the railroad tracks.*
>
> *After listening to us kids complain about how hot and miserable we were, Mama finally decided we should go inside the store where Daddy was. Now we stood waiting for him just inside Castleberry's, where the pungent odor of fertilizers and pesticides overpowered the scent of freshly mown grass.*

How did the senses help set the mood?

PROVIDE READER WITH THE BASICS

When telling any story, fiction or memoir, the writer should answer these basic questions for the reader:

Who or what?
When?
Where?
Why?
How?

And with memoir, it's a good idea to answer two additional questions:

How did the experience make you feel?

Did you learn something from it? If so, what?

SHOW—AND TELL!

Fiction writers are told, "Show. Don't tell."—and you *do* want your memoir to read like a novel, right? Right. But with memoir, you are not just telling a story to entertain; you are also writing about how you became the person you are—what shaped you. Your feelings, hopes, dreams, and disappointments are important to memoir. So you should show AND tell.

If you're writing about your mother, for example, don't just *tell* us she loved you. Prove it by showing what she did or said that made you believe she loved you. Also, tell how her actions affected you. Does the following passage do both?

Whenever Mama noticed me yawning or nodding off during the preaching service, she would lean me over until my head rested in her lap. As I lay stretched out on the hard, wooden pew, Mama would stroke my hair and tug at my curls—perhaps absentmindedly—wrapping strands around her fingers, then stretching each ringlet to its full length before letting it spring back. Mama's touch gave me a warm feeling all over and always put me right to sleep.

VIVID DESCRIPTION

Many years ago, I took a writing class taught by Bill Maxwell, a former opinion columnist for the *St. Petersburg Times*. (I've always admired his ability to write clearly about complex subjects such as social injustice.) In the class, Mr. Maxwell held up a drawing of Humpty Dumpty sitting on a stone wall.

All I saw was the wall and Humpty Dumpty on top of it, his back to me. Maxwell told us that writers are like Humpty Dumpty. They see beyond the wall, and it's the writer's duty to convey the scene in such a way that the reader sees it too.

Description is also important when it comes to objects mentioned in your stories. Author Stephen King writes about this in his book, *On Writing*, saying never generalize when you can be specific. Which example below says more in less space?

> The boy kicked the can down the famous highway.
> Ben kicked the Pepsi can along Route 66.

In classes I teach, we complete an exercise that helps writers recognize the importance of providing precise details. It's a bit like the games of Charades and Pictionary, but with words instead of pantomiming and drawing. Beforehand, I place common household items in paper sacks, one item per sack, with enough sacks for everyone to have one. Each sack might contain an apple, a belt, brooch, pen, keychain, golf tee—anything that will fit inside it.

The item is not to be removed, but each person looks into his/her sack, and without saying the name of the item, writes a description. They use visual and sensory details to describe what's in the sack (the apple and the leather belt, for example, would each have a distinct scent). Students then read their descriptions to the class to see if they provided enough visual and sensory details for others to identify the objects.

PHYSICAL DESCRIPTIONS OF PEOPLE

If you say a person is pretty, what does that really tell your reader? Not much. You must provide words that create an image in the reader's mind.

As a youngster, living on a farm in North Florida, I was in awe of the way my Miami grandmother dressed. I could have said just that: "I was in awe of the way my Miami grandmother dressed." But I wanted others to see her as I did, so I wrote:

> *Although I saw my Miami grandmother only once a year, I looked at pictures of her year 'round. I liked the deckled-edged photo of her and Granddaddy in which he sported an all-white suit, and Grandma, standing*

next to him, wore a dark fitted suit that showed off her slender figure.

When she visited us each summer, though, she packed only lightweight dresses, made of soft rayon, that draped in pleats and tucks, and swirled when she walked. If she wore accessories, she chose a strand of pearls, a gold pin—or a white hanky tucked into a breast pocket, so only the hankie's lace edges overflowed. When I could buy my own clothes, I wanted to dress exactly like my Miami grandmother and wear high heels, like hers, with tiny toe cutouts.

If we have photos of those we describe, we can include the pictures, too.

DESCRIBING PERSONALITY AND CHARACTER

When it comes to personality and character, though, words must do all the work. And providing insight into your character's personality is even more important than physical description. In Jim Huber's funny and poignant memoir, *I 'member one time . . .* , he wrote this about his father:

> *If I had to describe my father in a single word, that word would be "distant." If I had to guess at his feelings for me, the word would be "tolerant." I never thought that my father loved me or really felt any affection for me at all. I was one of many—thirteen— for whom he had to somehow provide, and I'm pretty sure that I, during my growing-up years, never did*

32

anything that made him pleased or proud or otherwise glad of the sacrifices he'd made on my behalf.

And he did make sacrifices. Though he liked beer, he almost never drank. He smoked Marvel cigarettes ("Worth crowing about!") which sold for 15¢ a pack (Camels, Lucky Strikes and Chesterfields were 21¢ a pack); grew his own vegetables; hauled his own trash to the landfill; worked as many overtime hours as were available; and wore his Oshkosh B'Gosh overalls until they were threadbare and the original blue had turned nearly white.

Perhaps you think that those aren't "Mother Theresa" level sacrifices. And you're right, they aren't. But please understand that I'm trying hard to make my dad a sympathetic character and, for most of my life, I didn't feel that he was.

What did you learn about the father's character?

What did you learn about the author?

AUTHENTIC DIALOGUE

The use of dialogue can add "air" to long passages of prose, and it can bring a story to life. You needn't worry that you don't remember remarks verbatim. Just write the gist of what was said. Do I remember what the shoe salesman said to me in "The Last Pair" on page 90? Of course not. It is my best recollection from fifty years ago.

Keep in mind that people talk in spurts. Overly long sentences won't ring true. Also, go easy on slang, heavy accents, and dialect. "I'z ain't gwine aks fer nothin' mo," slows the reader because it's difficult to read. Alter the spelling of only a few choice words, and you still get the dialect: "I ain't gwine ask for nothin' more."

IMAGES, LETTERS, MEMORABILIA

If you have images, letters, receipts, and other memorabilia that will enhance your memoir, include them, along with captions. In *C.G. & Ethel: A Family History,* I included over a hundred photographs and numerous letters, such as the one below, to help tell the story.

This one was written by my mother's brother, who lied about his age when he was sixteen so he could join the War Department. His goal? To send his paychecks home so his parents could replace their old log home with one with electricity—at a time when power lines did not extend to their neck of the woods.

5/18/43
A.P.O. 869
Miami, Fla.

Hello Mama, and Daddy,
      How are you, and the rest of the family? I am still working, and eating, and I feel fine too.
      Well I guess you have your new cookers for the tobacco barn by now, and what do you think of them. I am sure you will

like them when you start using it, no more sleepless nights, and boy that is something.

Listen when you find out if you can build a house, why don't you look at some plans, and pick out one just like you want, and let him figure with you on it, and see if he will bring it under the F.H.A. for us. If he will, it will be better for him and for us, and if he can't we will see what else we can do. If the F.H.A. will handle it we can buy new furniture and a lot of other things we need. If not we will buy it outright. Don't forget the tile floors, and walls for the kitchen, and put it in a position where we can build a nice garage beside it. We are going to make that a beautiful place.

Listen Daddy look in the catalogue, and see about a Delco system, and figure up the number of lights you will have in the house, and all electrical appliances you will have including the pump, and see what [a] plant will cost that will handle it, and get the easy payment rate for the engine, and pump, and the batteries. If it is not too much we will go ahead and order it, and then we will have that. We want an automatic load control too, don't we?

I guess you think I'm silly to write all this crap, but I want to help plan for this dream home.

Well I am not sending a check home this week for I lost a lot of time on account of rain, and I am buying a radio for company as there is no place to go very much.

Well I am going to close for this time as I am getting sleepy, so write real soon and all the news.

Lots of love,
Harold Rye

HOW LONG SHOULD A MEMOIR BE?

Most memoirs are between 65,000 and 90,000 words, but there are no rules. Calvin Trillin's memoir *About Alice,* a bestseller, is only 25,000 words, whereas Jeannette Walls's *The Glass Castle*, another bestseller, is about 100,000 words.

For now, don't worry about length. Just write the stories you want to write. Keep this in mind, however: just because an event happened doesn't mean it should go into your memoir. Before you include the story, ask yourself these questions:

1. Does this incident tell the reader something important about me, the situation, or the culture in which I lived?

2. Will this episode move my story forward or bog it down?

When you begin writing about a topic, stay focused. If you find yourself veering onto another subject, stop and ask yourself: *Should I write another story that focuses on this new topic?* If you write something that doesn't really fit within your memoir, don't discard it. It may have a different purpose. And likely, every story you write will be treasured by those who love you.

As time goes on, consider giving a story as a birthday gift or for some other occasion. It is especially exciting to a child to read what someone has written about his/her birth or a special occasion when the child made someone proud. Also, if you write about a person who has passed away, you might wish to give a copy to the deceased person's loved ones. They would, no doubt, treasure it.

Consider submitting stories to magazines or literary journals, too, such as *Bacopa* or *Glimmer Train*. The NewPages website lists magazines and literary journals that accept unsolicited submissions: *http://www.newpages.com/magazines/*

If you plan to publish your memoir through a traditional publisher, having been published elsewhere will be a real plus.

Exercise 3.3 — Write using a memory wheel

Write a story using a memory wheel you've created of a person. Do not stop to edit, but do try to employ the elements mentioned in this chapter (vivid description, authentic dialogue, and how the person made you feel.). Provide not only physical descriptions, but insight into the person's character and personality. If applicable, include what you learned from the person, good or bad.

Complete the Adolescence Questionnaire, p. 71.

4

Writing Past Fear

Exercise 4.1 — Six major turning points in your life

Think back over your life. Pinpoint six pivotal moments and write them down. Did any of these turning points include an emotionally charged experience? If so, write about it.

In Chapter 1, we looked at the reasons we postponed writing about our lives. For some, procrastination had to do with time. But for many of us, it was more about fear. Fear that we might reveal we're poor grammarians or poor writers; fear of embarrassing ourselves and/or our families; fear of boring the reader, of revealing too much, of being vulnerable, of airing dirty laundry, of reliving unpleasant events, of hurting others.

If you're afraid your writing isn't up to snuff, remember that, for now, you are writing a draft, for yourself only. As Tristine Rainer states in her book, *Your Life as Story*, feel free to write a really shitty first draft.

Writing about embarrassing experiences or painful episodes can be cathartic for us and helpful to others. Keep in mind that most readers don't seek out books about perfect people who have led perfect lives. As Abigail Thomas wrote in her book, *Thinking About Memoir*, "Dig deep, or don't bother."

> *"Dig deep, or don't bother."*
>
> —Abigail Thomas

If you were to Google the phrase "What makes a good book?" you'd find lots of answers: books that teach me something, books with well-developed characters, books with action, books with surprise endings, books with humor, books that make me cry.

Above all, readers want the author to make them *feel* something. And to make a reader *feel*, the author needs to go beyond telling a tale equivalent to a sunny day at the park. Keep these points in mind as you write:

- Tell the reader what and who had a profound effect on you. How did it happen?
- Provide exquisite detail so the reader "sees" events in your life unfold.
- If you write about both your childhood and your adult years, include the same vivid details in each.
- Include drama—conflict, disabilities, death. What was your reaction to these?
- Don't try to reinvent yourself.
- Be as truthful as possible and don't omit what you are ashamed of.

Reread the last point: *Be as truthful as possible and don't omit what you are ashamed of.* Show the reader you are a human being who makes mistakes and learns from them.

Earlier, you wrote a page, beginning each line with "I remember feeling" followed by a tactile sensation such as "the hot sand on St. Augustine Beach." Now complete the following exercise that focuses on emotional feelings that were unpleasant.

Exercise 4.2 — I remember feeling . . .

Fill a page with a different feeling on each line. For example:

> I remember feeling hurt when accused of stealing . . .
> I remember feeling the sting of Daddy's belt on my. . .
> I remember feeling angry because . . .
> I remember feeling overwhelmed when . . .
> I remember feeling stupid because . . .
> I remember feeling apprehensive about . . .
> I remember feeling disgust for . . .
> I remember feeling hatred toward . . .
> I remember . . .

Few people reach adulthood without experiencing a few painful emotional or traumatic events. Some of these may be difficult to write about.

TACKLING EMBARRASSING/PAINFUL EXPERIENCES
Sometimes we must ease into difficult topics by writing about them in different ways. Here are suggestions:

- Write humorously
- Write in third person
- Write the story as a fairytale
- Write the tale as fiction
- Write the story as a limerick

When I wrote my first memoir story, it had to do with my wetting the bed and being punished for it. The experience was painful for me to recall; I felt ashamed and self-conscious about it. I also felt I was betraying my mother for saying she punished me for something I couldn't help. My writing mentor suggested that I write the tale as a limerick, so I wrote:

There once was a girl named Sue
Whose bad habit they all knew
Pee in the pot, she did not.
Pee on the cot? She did thot!
Till her Mommy became coo-coo!

Writing the experience as a limerick—putting humor into the situation—opened the door for me. I was able to face this humiliating experience and eventually write in more detail. In fact, my bedwetting habit became the focus of my first childhood memoir—the obstacle I wanted most to overcome.

Exercise 4.3 — Write a limerick

Exercise 4.3 — Write a limerick

Limericks are five lines and have an AABBA rhyme scheme, which means the first, second, and last lines (A) rhyme with each other, while the third and fourth lines (B) rhyme with one another. Introduce the character in the first line.

If you need help with words that rhyme, check out this website: *http://www.rhymezone.com*

What about being molested or abused, physically or emotionally as a child? How do we write about that? Keep in mind that, as children, we had little control over our lives; we looked up to those who were older. Even if the abuse occurred after you were an adult, you were the victim.

It might help, when you first begin to write, to distance yourself from abuse by writing in third person. Instead of writing, "My uncle pulled me in close, and as he hugged me tight, placed his hand on . . . ." You might say, "Her uncle pulled her in close, hugged her tight, and placed his hand . . . ." Or write the first draft as a fairy tale and cast the offending party as a rodent or snake.

> *"Autobiography is not to be trusted unless it reveals something disgraceful."*
>
> — George Orwell

WHAT ABOUT HURTING OTHERS?

This can happen. When my mother read the story I'd written about her punishing me for wetting the bed, she apologized for punishing me. But she accepted that the story was important for me to include in my memoir because of the profound effect the experience had on me.

Likewise, when my father read a chapter I wrote about his whipping me with a leather belt, he wanted me to leave that part out. I explained that if the book were all peaches and cream, it wouldn't be real; besides, the discipline helped make me who I am today. He agreed that I could leave it.

AVOIDING TROUBLE

Writers of memoir sometimes ask: "Can I get into trouble for revealing faults about others?" You bet! But you might phrase what you have to say in such a way that you plant the idea without actually stating fact. For example:

> *"I wouldn't call him a jerk, but he could be difficult."*
> *"I wouldn't say he was stupid, but . . ."*
> *"I heard such and such, but I'm sure it was only gossip."*

That should lessen your chances of having someone become angry at you, but it doesn't guarantee it.

Marjorie Kinnan Rawlings, who won a Pulitzer for *The Yearling*, was sued for libel by a neighbor she wrote about in *Cross Creek*. Rawlings had written that Zelma Cason, her neighbor, was . . .

an ageless spinster resembling an angry and efficient canary. She manages her orange grove and as much of the village and county as needs management or will submit to it. I cannot decide whether she should have been a man or a mother . . .

The plaintiff won the case, though the judge awarded her only one dollar in damages, plus court costs.

In the biography of my parents, I offended a descendant of a person mentioned in the book because I'd referred to a young woman's out-of-wedlock baby as a "bastard child." I'd heard adults use that term to describe the baby when I was growing up. But the granddaughter of this child loved her grandmother very much, and hearing her referred to in that manner upset her. She confronted me at a book signing. I agreed to remove the offensive term when I reprinted the book. She was grateful, thanking me for that and for including in the book a photograph of the man who'd fathered her grandmother. She'd never seen a picture of him.

Lucky for me, I wasn't sued. The woman who gave birth to the out-of-wedlock child had passed away, and her granddaughter couldn't sue because what I'd written wasn't about her. Still, I was truly sorry I had offended anyone.

Don't make my mistake. Do give thought to how something you write will come across to those closer to the situation. If what you write could be offensive, you may wish to use anonymous names. You could go even further by changing the description to make the person unrecognizable.

You might give the person characteristics or attributes they don't have. I think it was writer Anne Lamott, who said in her excellent book *Bird by Bird,* to give an abusive man in your story a teeny penis, saying he'd never sue because he'd never admit to having that physical attribute.

Author Mary Cameron Kilgour, a foreign-service officer during Bill Clinton's administration, wrote about her painful childhood experiences in her memoir, *Me May Mary.* She changed the names of everyone in the book except her family. In the book's preface, she states, "Other people won't recognize these people but they will recognize themselves."

Complete the Adult Years Questionnaire, p. 75.

5

Wrapping It Up

STAYING MOTIVATED

The ongoing solitary process of writing can be lonely. You may feel a high when you complete a story, then a low when you can't get another tale to flow as you'd like. And if you have no deadlines set for yourself, how do you keep going, especially when there is no instant gratification—no payment and no adulation—for your hard work?

The answer for many is to join a writing group. Call your local library and inquire about such a group. Check the newspaper. Talk with friends.

> *"Successful writers are not the ones who write the best sentences. They are the ones who keep writing. They are the ones who . . . keep believing in the value of their work, despite the difficulties."*
>
> —**Bonnie Friedman**

Find a group that meets regularly so you'll have constant deadlines. The group should be one where you receive positive support and honest feedback on your work. If you find it impossible to join a writing group, make a commitment to yourself to write at least one story each week until you can connect with other writers. Even better if you can write one story a day.

CONTINUE TO DIG INTO THE PAST

Talk with siblings, relatives, friends, former teachers and neighbors about the past. Consider any and all sources that might revive old memories:

- Visit towns you've lived in.
- Visit cemeteries, the courthouse, town hall.
- Check with the local chamber of commerce and area museums.
- Check newspaper archives.
- Peruse old family photographs.
- Look through your collection of recipes.
- Go to reunions (family, church, school).
- Look at diplomas and review school yearbooks.
- Look through bills, receipts, newspaper clippings, ledgers.
- Reread old letters.
- Check the family Bible and old address books.
- Review your Social Security Statement.

Your Social Security Statement will show the amount on which you paid Social Security each year. You may request a copy by completing form #7004. It's available online at: *https://www.ssa.gov/myaccount/SSA-7004.pdf*

If you have specific questions you'd like to ask others, write or email them and ask for a written reply. That way you'll have their exact words if you decide to quote them. If you do that, though, it's a good idea to ask permission.

PERMISSIONS

Get permission to use any and all material you did not write or that does not belong to you (e.g., letters, photographs, long excerpts from other books). If you publish for monetary gain, your publisher will require it. And it's the right thing to do. Obtain permission for all borrowed material, even if you self-publish only a few copies for family and friends.

GENEALOGY

Inquire if relatives have done genealogy research and, if so, whether they would share the research with you. But I do not recommend that you begin your own genealogy research while writing your memoir. Writing memoir can be a full-time job, and the same goes for genealogy research.

REMEMBERING TRIVIAL YET NOTABLE DETAILS

Remember to include details of your daily routine, health care, relationships, marriage, career, food preparations, shopping, etc. The fact that your first grocery bill in 1950 came to $11.21 might seem trivial to you now, but facts such as this grow in historic importance over time.

BELIEFS AND VALUES

Discuss your spiritual or religious beliefs and your values, as well as your hopes, dreams, and illusions. But interweave these with your experiences. Few people like to read books that preach. Let your stories—the examples you've set and what you've learned from your experiences—speak for you. Hm-m-m. It occurs to me that I sound as if I'm *preaching* now, since I'm saying "do this" and "do that." So, I'll provide an example to illustrate the next point about verifying facts.

VERIFY FACTS

I once wrote that "a bluebird was building a nest in a small shrub next to the porch." My sister, a born naturalist, pointed out my error, saying, "Bluebirds don't build nests in shrubs." My research revealed that she was right. Bluebirds build their nests several feet off the ground in abandoned woodpecker holes or other natural cavities that provide protection—or in bluebird houses we humans build for them.

For our work to have credibility, we must verify known facts. If you're unsure of your memory and your research fails to provide the answer, what do you do? Consider using a phrase such as "I can't be sure, but . . . "

REVIEWING YOUR FIRST DRAFT

Don't waste time trying to edit when you still have lots of stories yet to write. Just keep pouring your heart onto the page. Let each draft rest a few days. Later, go back and ask yourself questions such as these:

- Am I clearly identifying my relatives? Your great grandchildren might like to know if Aunt Lizzy was on your father's side or your mother's side.

- Are there places where dialogue could replace narrative? Actual conversations make your book come alive.

- Are my sentences as concise and to the point as they could be? Tight writing is almost always better writing.

- Have I provided insight into my feelings? For example, if I stated that Aunt Oleta was my favorite aunt, did I explain why? Did I provide a story to support my feelings?

ORGANIZING YOUR STORIES

After you've written a number of stories, you should begin to: (1) have a feel for what aspect of your life or how much of your life you wish to cover in this memoir (e.g., childhood, job, children, passion, etc.) and (2) identify your memoir's theme.

REVISING AND REWRITING

With a theme in mind, place the pieces you've written in the order that works best. Then decide if you want to publish the stories as stand-alone pieces or weave them together so your book will feel like a novel. If the latter, you'll want to revise and rewrite to tie the stories together. This may require cutting some stories and adding others to fill in gaps.

Theodore A. Rees Cheney, in his book *Getting the Words Right: How to Revise, Edit and Rewrite,* stresses the importance of ensuring that every word, sentence, and paragraph advances the theme or plot.

Give careful attention to the beginning—what story and which sentence will come first. Most successful novels have a hook to pull the reader in. Good memoirs do too.

> *"Write your first draft with your heart. Rewrite with your head."*
>
> — from *Finding Forrester*

Assuming that something of importance happens in your memoir—that some longing is resolved or that some goal is achieved—consider hinting at this in your opening sentence, but never give away your ending.

EDITING

When you've completed all your stories or chapters and revised or rewritten as needed, it's time to edit. This is when participation in a writing group becomes critical. As you prepare to submit your chapters to members of the group, make improvements such as these:

- Eliminate clichés (high as a mountain, cute as a button, bright eyed and bushytailed). Come up with your own original phrases.

- Eliminate "I remember" or "I thought." Those phrases helped you to recall events but are unnecessary in your final manuscript since *the entire book* is what you remember or think.

- Change passive verbs to active where possible. For example, "At birth, I was named Joe Lee" could be made active: "At birth, my parents named me Joe Lee."

  The following website will help you identify "to be" verbs: *http://www.aztekera.com/tools/tobeverbs.php*

- Eliminate fluff. See how many "ly" adverbs can be eliminated by using stronger verbs. "She walked slowly" might be "She ambled." Don't worry that deleting unnecessary adverbs and adjectives will make your memoir too short. If you write concisely but with feeling and adequate descriptive detail about relevant experiences, you will end up with an interesting memoir. Length is not what's important.

  To see if your writing is as lean as it could be, run a sample through The Writer's Diet website: *http://writersdiet.com/?page_id=4*

- Ask yourself if each word, sentence, paragraph, or chapter moves your story forward. If not, delete it. But save the piece; you might be able to use it later in some other way.

Keep a good dictionary and thesaurus on hand. Use the dictionary to check spelling, but don't rule out colloquial and familiar language. Be careful when you edit that you don't lose *your voice,* which is one element that will make your book unique. Proper English may not say it as well as slang. When

I wet the bed as a kid, for example, should I have said I "urinated" or I "peed" on the bed? Keep in mind the words used at a particular age.

Never ever use a thesaurus to look up pompous or flowery words just to impress readers. Your writing won't sound authentic. Instead, use a thesaurus to locate words that better describe what you wish to say or to give variety.

Exercise 5.1 — Make proper use of a good thesaurus

Look at the following sentence, and after consulting a thesaurus, see how you might improve the sentence by making the adjective *little* more precise:

> *When I was a little girl, Daddy built me a little doll house, complete with a little cupboard where I could store and play with my little tea set.*

If you have concerns about grammar or sentence structure, refer to Strunk & White's: *The Elements of Style*. Also, Patricia O'Conner's *Woe Is I* is a good reference and fun to read, but make note that O'Conner is a Brit and uses the British style of punctuation. American style calls for *all* commas and periods to be placed within quotation marks.

Recommended websites for grammar and writing questions:

> *https://owl.english.purdue.edu/owl/*
> *http://www.quickanddirtytips.com/grammargirl*

Most traditional publishers use *The Chicago Manual of Style.* If you plan to submit your final manuscript to a publisher, use that manual as your style reference.

Finally, read your stories aloud. If certain combinations of words cause you to stutter or stumble, revise the words. Try taping yourself and play it back to hear how the overall story sounds.

WHAT SHOULD YOU NOT EDIT

While it is acceptable to correct another person's grammar and punctuation in quoted material, it may be better to leave it "as is." In *C.G. & Ethel: A Family History,* I refrained from editing a poem written by my Miami grandmother, the person I described in Chapter 3—the one I wanted to dress exactly like when I grew up.

She had not always been able to dress so elegantly, not when she was a widow with a seventh-grade education, share-cropping to provide for her seven children.

After my father passed away at the age of ninety, I found a tattered piece of paper in his wallet. The paper had been folded and refolded so many times it almost fell apart as I opened it. On it was a poem he had evidently kept since he'd graduated from high school, the first in his family to do so. The poem was signed by his mother (my Miami grand-mother). When I included the poem in the biography mentioned above, I changed nothing:

A Mother's Dream Come True

Heres to my boy who would never say die,
But who's watchword was ever, I'll try.
To fight my way to Victory,
And justify man's faith in me.

Hard has been the battle,
Dark has been the way;
But, now for you, the sun is shining
For you won the fight today.

With your school-mates you are standing
While teachers look on with pride
On this class of '37,
Their faith in you is justified.

On this, your day of graduation
With Diploma in your hand
And with other hard-won medals
You upon the stage do stand.

On your brow a look of Peace,
Fiery determination in your eye
To surmount every future Obstacle,
Be them ever so high.

In my heart is songs of gladness
Of your victory, justly won,
In my eyes, tears of happiness,
As I clasp your hand, My son:

Boy, on this day, which means so much to you,
Saw a mother's dream come true.

My father didn't complete high school until he was twenty-one years of age, having had to drop out of school to help his widowed mother with the farming. No wonder she was proud of his accomplishment.

PREPARING TO PUBLISH YOUR WORK

Ask three to five neutral individuals (not family or close friends) to serve as your Beta readers—to read your work all the way through and give you objective feedback. When you receive their comments and suggestions, carefully consider what they said, especially if two readers said the same thing.

But again, be careful that you don't lose your unique voice. In the book, *The Forest for the Trees: An Editor's Advice to Writers*, author Betsy Lerner states: "Give up the hope that people will like your work. People like vanilla ice cream. Hope that they love your work or hate it. That they find it exquisite or revolting."

She goes on to quote the French author, artist, and film director Jean Cocteau who said, "Note just what it is about your work that the critics don't like and cultivate it. That's the only part of your work that's individual and worth keeping." I don't totally agree with Lerner and Cocteau, but you do need to evaluate the feedback you receive.

Sometime you will receive conflicting comments. What one reviewer loves, another despises. Ultimately, you are the author, and you must make the final decisions about what to keep and what to delete, down to the punctuation.

Front matter: Look at professionally published books to see how the front matter is arranged. There are many variations, but here's a fairly standard format:

Blank page (optional)
Title page
Half title page (optional)
Copyright page
Dedication (optional)
Acknowledgments (optional)
Table of Contents (page numbers are optional)
Preface

Final considerations:

- **Book title**–Your title is your first hook. What will yours be? Lulu.com offers a free service to rate titles. Try it for fun: *http://www.lulu.com/titlescorer/*

- **Cover and binding**–Hardbacks are more expensive than paperbacks but more durable.

- **Images**–Will you include photos, drawings, charts? If so, will they be interspersed throughout the text or collected at the end of your book?

- **Paper**–Choose acid-free paper stock to withstand time; standard weight is 55 lb.

- **Permissions**–If you have not done so already, obtain written permission for any and all borrowed material such as photos, poems, songs, book excerpts.

WAYS TO PUBLISH

If you are not a celebrity and a publisher approaches you about publishing your book, it's probably a scam. It is definitely a scam if the publisher asks you for money up front. Don't fall for it.

And you should never pay an agent. Agents have the option of shopping your manuscript to publishers, and if they succeed in placing your book with a publisher, they will receive a percentage of your royalties. If an agent asks for money up front, run!

How you choose which route to take when it comes to publishing depends on (1) whether you wish to print a few copies for family and friends or expect to sell thousands, and (2) how much time you can devote to the process. Do you have the time and expertise, for example, to hire editors, to purchase the ISBN,[1] register copyright, etc.

1. True self-publishing

With true self-publishing, you handle all aspects of publishing including editing, design, proofreading, hiring the printer, obtaining the ISBN, registering the copyright, marketing, distribution, etc. All royalties belong to you, the author. You pay all costs, including printing and binding, and you set your own sales price. A drawback is that you may find it impossible to get a bookstore to carry your book, so you become the sole salesperson.

---

[1] ISBN stands for International Standard Book Number. These are obtained from Bowker: *http://www.bowker.com/products/ISBN-US.html.*

2. Print-on-demand (POD) self-publishing

This type of self-publishing is rapidly gaining in popularity. Kindle Direct Publishing (KDP), an Amazon company, is perhaps the most popular POD publisher. KDP began as a publisher of e-books for Kindle, but later merged with Amazon's CreateSpace to publish paperbacks. If you want your book to have a hardcover, check out Ingram Spark and Lighting Source (the parent company is Ingram), which offers hardcover, softcover and e-books.

With most POD publishers, you may edit and format the book yourself, hire someone to do it, or pay the POD publisher to do this. When you are ready to publish, you may obtain your own ISBN or let the publisher supply it. You can design a cover using a number of templates provided by the publisher or supply your own design, so long as it meets the publisher's specifications.

You download a digital file of your manuscript to the publisher's server. After the publisher reviews the file to make sure the text fits within the margins, that the images are of sufficient resolution (300 dpi), etc., you may order a proof copy to review. Within a few days after you approve the proof, your book will appear in distribution channels (e.g., your KDP book will appear on Amazon; your Ingram Sparks or Lightning Source book will be available through Barnes and Noble and other outlets).

3. Vanity or subsidy publishing

You choose a "package" that may include editing, marketing, etc., and pay a fee for the services you select. The publisher obtains and own the ISBN, sets the price, publishes the book, and may offer to get it into distribution channels. These companies keep a higher percentage of royalties than POD publishers.

If you just want to print a few copies for family and friends, and want a hardcover book, this may be the way to go. But before you choose this route, ask questions: What are the upfront costs? Where do you distribute? What will be my royalties? Will I retain copyright?

4. Traditional/trade publishers

At this time, the big-five trade publishers are Hachette, HarperCollins, Macmillan, Penguin Random House, and Simon & Schuster. They provide editing, marketing, and distribution. They pay royalties of around 10%. They are highly selective about what they publish, and usually work exclusively through agents.

5. Small presses

Small presses and regional publishers (e.g., Ampersand Books, Pineapple Press, University Press of Florida) act much like traditional publishers, but they are approachable—you do not need an agent. The *Poets & Writers* website lists a number of small presses: *http://www.pw.org/small_presses/*

DECIDING WHICH ROUTE TO TAKE

The Science Fiction and Fantasy Writers of America's website provides numerous tips and caveats that apply to all authors: *http://www.sfwa.org/other-resources/for-authors/*. Check it out. Also look through professionally published books to find one with formatting you like (margins, font, etc.).

Think about your publishing goals—how many copies you expect to sell—before deciding which route to take. Then check out the website of the publisher you want to use and read the company's guidelines. A small press, for example, will require a double-spaced manuscript, whereas a POD publisher will expect the manuscript to be formatted for print when you download the digital file. Whatever is requested, follow the publisher's guidelines exactly.

THE KEY TO SUCCESS

As with any skill, your writing will become better with practice. Innate talent is nice to have, but perseverance is key. It's not always the most talented person who succeeds. It is the one who perseveres—the one who believes in the value of the work and keeps moving toward a set goal.

> *"Hard work beats talent when talent doesn't work hard."*
>
> —Tim Tebow

Best wishes as you work toward your goal!

Susie

APPENDIX

Early Childhood Questionnaire

The name _____

was given to me at birth because _____.

I think of my mother as _____ and _____.

As a preschooler, my favorite toy was _____.

I would describe my relationship with my siblings (or cousins) as

_____.

My father was the _____of our family

and if I had to describe him in one word, it would be _____.

When I was sick with _____, I remember wishing

that _____.

When I was really little, I liked to play _____.

Before I started school, my favorite place was _____.

The first friend I ever had was _____, who lived

_____.

I wonder whatever happened to the man/woman by the name of

_____ who lived _____.

My favorite pet, _____, would _____.

At age 8, the occasion that got me most excited was _____.

When I was ___, I wanted to learn to _____

like _____ because _____.

One of our neighbors, _____, was always _____.

The program I liked best on the radio or TV was_____

because _____.

One of the first books I remember enjoying was _____.

I remember my first experience with death was _____

_____.

At the age of _____, I wanted to grow up to become _____.

The one thing I will never forget is _____.

I am most proud of _____

because _____.

Early Schooldays Questionnaire

My best friend in _____ grade was _____.

The most fun we had together was when we _____

_____.

I was very different from my (sibling/best friend), _____

who liked to _____.

He/she sometimes got into trouble for _____.

I remember getting into trouble once for _____.

I once got punished for _____.

My favorite teacher was _____

because _____.

My favorite subject was _____.

When I was _____ years old, I learned to _____

_____.

I felt alone and scared when I was _____

_____.

At home, I had to help my _____

with _____.

On Saturdays, I always _____

_____.

On Saturday nights, I _____.

Every Sunday, our family _____.

During summers, I _____.

My first kiss was with _____,

and it was _____.

I remember feeling _____

_____.

My grades were always _____.

I wanted to make a good impression on _____

because _____.

My mother didn't understand why I _____.

My father got really mad at me for _____.

At times, I just wanted to _____.

The person who helped me gain confidence in myself was _____

_____. He/she told me _____

_____.

Adolescence Questionnaire

In junior high school, my best friend was _____.

The most fun we ever had together was when we _____

_____.

I remember getting into trouble for _____.

My favorite teacher in junior high was _____

because _____.

My favorite subject in junior high was _____.

I felt alone and scared when _____.

_____.

By the time I was thirteen, I thought _____.

My favorite teacher in high school was _____

because _____.

One teacher made me feel _____

because he/she _____.

The subjects I enjoyed most in school were _____,

71

_____, and _____.

Subjects I disliked were _____,

and _____.

My extracurricular activities included _____

_____.

Being popular in high school was _____.

My favorite hangout was _____

because _____.

I liked to hang around with _____,

but _____.

The first thing anyone noticed about me was _____.

Friends said I was _____.

When I look back at pictures of myself at the age of 16, I think __

_____.

A person looking at me as a teenager now might think that I ____

_____.

My role model was _____.

The worst thing I ever did was _____.

I remember the time I didn't go to school because _____

_____.

I was most proud when I _____.

My first summer or after-school job was _____.

I was paid $_____ per _____.

The thing I liked most about that job was _____.

The thing I liked least was _____.

The movie I remember most vividly from my teenage years is ___

_____.

I never agreed with my parents about _____.

The person in my family I felt closest to was _____

because _____.

By the time I was 18, I thought _____.

I left home at the age of _____ to _____.

I had mixed feelings then about _____,

but I know now that _____.

If I could live my teenage years over again, I would _____

_____.

The accomplishment I am most proud of is _____

_____.

Adult Years Questionnaire

A typical day for me at the age of twenty was _____

_____.

When I turned twenty-one, I thought _____

_____.

The first election in which I voted was in (year) _____.

I voted for _____.

Politics today is _____.

The military played (or did not play) a role in my life because

_____.

The most fun I ever had was _____.

Once I was tricked into _____.

Turning thirty was _____.

The most important thing a parent can teach a child is _____

_____.

I didn't really feel that I was grown up until _____.

What I enjoyed most as a young adult was _____

_____.

There is still one thing I want to accomplish in my lifetime and it is

to _____.

The job that brought me the most satisfaction was _____

_____

because _____.

My motivation for becoming a _____ was

_____.

The person who helped me advance the most in my role as _____

_____ was _____

by _____.

I once worked with (or knew) a man/woman who _____

_____.

I have had several turning points in my life. The most important

was _____

_____.

I (almost) got fired once for _____.

The experience left me feeling _____.

Once, a co-worker told me _____.

The biggest compliment I ever received was from _____.

He/she said I _____.

Marriage to me means _____.

Children are _____.

I am proud of being _____.

The biggest move I ever made in my life was _____

_____.

At the age of _____, I felt that money was _____

_____.

Having money in my wallet now is _____.

Having money in the bank is _____.

Having more money than one needs is _____.

My biggest regret in life is that I _____.

I still want to learn to _____.

The person I wish I knew personally is _____.

The person I most admire in the world is _____

because _____.

The person who has influenced me the most is _____.

He/she taught me _____.

My career success came at the expense of _____.

If I could change one thing about me, it would be _____

_____.

The most famous person I ever met was _____

when _____.

If I could be famous for one thing now, it would be _____

_____.

What I want my family to remember about me is _____

_____.

A typical day now for me is _____

_____.

The thing they never teach you in school is _____

_____.

The incident that made me grow up the most was _____

_____.

The worst mistake I ever made was _____

_____.

The one thing that has caused the most conflict during my life is

_____.

I have received the most joy from _____.

I try to resolve differences by _____.

The most stressful time in my life was _____.

Divorce is _____.

In raising children, it is important to always _____.

I remember a trip to _____

which was _____.

Life has taught me _____.

The one thing I want *everyone* to know about me is _____

_____.

The one thing I want *no one* to know is _____

_____.

Questions to Oust Writer's Block

Cut questions apart; place in a jar to pull out when you need a prompt.

How would you describe yourself to someone
who doesn't know you?

For what are you most grateful? Why?

What were some of your favorite activities while growing up?

What would be your perfect day, real or fictional?

What have you learned about yourself in the past week?

What have you learned about yourself in the past year?

If you could have one wish come true, what would it be?

What is your favorite book and why?

Who were your mentors?

What is your favorite season? Why?

What color describes you best? In what way?

If you were to be reincarnated as an animal, which one would it be and why?

What is something that you have never told anyone?

What makes you laugh?

What rituals do you have in your life?

What was your most embarrassing moment ever?

What is your favorite holiday memory?

What was your happiest moment ever?

When were you most afraid?

What do you worry most about?

If you could pass along one good trait of yours to your children or grandchildren, what would it be? Why?

What is the one thing you wish you could change about yourself?

What have you not yet accomplished that you want to accomplish in your lifetime?

What talent are you most proud of?

What is your favorite time of day? Why?

If you could meet anyone, real or fictional, past or present, who would it be? Why?

Is there something you wish you could take back?

What is the best gift you have ever received? Why?

What is the best vacation you have ever experienced? And what is the vacation of your dreams?

How do you feel about your car and your home?

How have your feelings about your house or car changed over time?

What subject do you wish you knew more about and why?

If you were starting over, would you take a different path in life? Explain why you would or would not.

When you were a child, what did you think you would grow up to become? Did you realize your dream? Why or why not?

What habit do you want most to break and why?

Did you receive religious instruction as a child? Do your beliefs today differ from what you believed then? If so, how?

Sample Story

The Last Pair
by Susie Baxter

In the early '60s when I was in high school, I often window-shopped during my Saturday lunch break from Priest's dime store. I'd check out the merchandise displayed in every store along West Howard Street, even Gibbs and Fleets, stores I seldom set foot in. Mama said their high prices—posted on tiny squares of white cardboard beside the items—bordered on criminal. I wondered if the stores did that so people who couldn't afford the merchandise would stay out.

One day as I moseyed along West Howard Street, a pair of pink pumps caught my eye in the Gibbs' window. The leather looked luminous, like pink pearls. I imagined slipping my feet into those beautiful shoes with slender, medium-height heels. Price: $29.95. Ugh. Of my three-dollar-a-day salary, I took home $2.91. Ten days of work for those shoes? Actually, eleven, considering tax. Forget it! But back at work that afternoon, I couldn't get those shoes out of my head. I could almost smell the leather. I vowed not to spend a penny on anything else until I had saved enough to buy those shoes.

As the weeks passed and my collected earnings got closer and closer to the amount needed, I felt giddy with excitement. When the day arrived, I marched myself into the store and showed the salesman the shoe I wanted. "Size 8½," I told him.

"Sure. Please have a seat," he said, motioning to a nearby chair.

I sat as the man disappeared through a doorway. He returned with a box, sat on the stool in front of me, and removed tissue paper the shoes were wrapped in. *Even prettier up close.*

Using a silver shoe horn, the man helped slip my foot into the shoe. I loved the way it looked on my foot. But when I stood, with shoes on both feet, they felt much too tight.

"I think I need a size 9," I said, almost in a whisper.

I'd always been embarrassed about my big feet. Mine had outgrown my older sisters' hand-me-down shoes about the time I started first grade. By age ten, I wore the same size Daddy did: size 8½. He often teased me about my feet, saying things like "When you butcher them feet, I want the livers out of 'em"—as if my feet were big as cows. Other times, he'd say, "You'd be a lot taller if half your body wasn't lapped under," or "Your Mama can buy shoes for your sisters and you can wear their boxes."

Most years when Mama bought Easter shoes for us, she wanted us to choose white ones, saying they went with everything. But I thought white shoes called attention—made my feet appear larger—so I often ended up with black patent leather.

As I stood now looking down at the pink pumps, the salesman pressed the toe of one shoe and said, "I think you've got plenty of room there, and they'll stretch. They're all leather and you know leather stretches. You want to start out with 'em being pretty snug."

"Yes, Sir," I said, "but this one really hurts—my right foot is bigger. I think I need the size 9."

"This is the last pair we have," he said. "It's the end of summer, so our fall shoes are coming in now—but remember—these *will* give! They'll stretch. And they look really nice on your feet."

The last pair? Well, that changed everything. They did look nice. No. They looked fabulous, and as the salesman kept assuring and reassuring me, I started believing every word he said.

At the counter, I plopped down the cash.

The next morning, I wore the new shoes to church. My feet had never looked so pretty. But during the church service, every time the choir director raised her arm, indicating the congregation should stand to sing, I cringed. The shoes were definitely too tight, and the soles were now scuffed—too late to return them.

I was determined to wear those shoes. Every few days, I'd try wearing them around the house to stretch them. It didn't work. Finally, I admitted to Mama that the shoes I'd bought were too tight.

"I think Millage Howard can stretch shoes," Mama said. "Why don't you take them to his shoe repair shop?"

I did as Mama suggested, but it didn't work.

Maybe Millage didn't leave the stretchers in long enough, I thought. So, when I heard of shoe stretchers you could buy and use at home, I purchased a set. I put them in the shoes, turned the little whacha-ma-gig as tight as I could twist it, and left the stretchers in the shoes a whole week.

They still hurt my feet.

From time to time over the next months and then years, I'd try wearing the shoes, thinking maybe I didn't remember correctly—maybe they weren't as tight as I recalled. I'd put them on, only to realize my memory was quite accurate.

My hopefulness continued until the liners inside the shoes became so brittle with age that they curled into a fetal position. Still not giving up, I got out a bottle of glue one day to secure the liner back in place. As I held it in place, I noticed the writing on the inside of the shoe. *Size 8.*

Date written 2/13/17

898 words

Bibliography

Barrington, Judith: *Writing the Memoir*

Charpentier, Patricia: *Eating an Elephant: Write Your Life One Bite at a Time*

Cheney, Theodore A. Rees: *Getting the Words Right: How to Revise, Edit and Rewrite*

Friedman, Bonnie: *Writing Past Dark*

Clark, Peter Roy: *Writing Tools: 55 Essential Strategies for Every Writer*

Daniel, Lois: *How to Write Your Own Life Story*

Goldberg, Natalie: *Writing Down the Bones: Freeing the Writer Within*

Dillard, Annie: *The Writing Life*

Hampl, Patricia: *I Could Tell You Stories: Sojourns in the Land of Memory*

Johnson, Alexandra: *Leaving a Trace*

Karls, John B.: *The Writer's Handbook, A Guide to the Essentials of Good Writing*

King, Stephen: *On Writing*

Lamott, Anne: *Bird by Bird: Some Instructions on Writing and Life*

Lerner, Betsy: *The Forest for the Trees: An Editor's Advice to Writers*

Rainer, Tristine: *Your Life as Story*

Ross, Hilda K: *Writing Your Life History: A Journey of Self-Discovery*

Stanek, Lou Willett: *Writing Your Life: Putting Your Past on Paper*

Thomas, Abigail: *Thinking About Memoir*

Zinsser, William: *Inventing the Truth*

Zousmer, Steve: *You Don't Have to Be Famous: How to Write Your Life Story*

Resources

Authors:
http://www.sfwa.org/other-resources/for-authors/

Autobiography and memoir:
http://www.centerautobio.org/autobiographic-writing/

Grammar and punctuation:
https://owl.english.purdue.edu/owl/
http://www.quickanddirtytips.com/grammargirl

Grammar and style:
Strunk & White: *The Elements of Style*
The Chicago Manual of Style

ISBN:
http://www.bowker.com/products/ISBN-US.html

Lean-writing test:
http://writersdiet.com/?page_id=4

Magazines and journals that publish memoir:
http://www.newpages.com/magazines/

Rhyming words:
http://www.rhymezone.com

Small presses:
http://www.pw.org/small_presses/

Social Security Statement of Earnings:
https://www.ssa.gov/myaccount/SSA-7004.pdf

Timelines:
Bernard Grun: *The Timetables of History*

Title scorer:
http://www.lulu.com/titlescorer/

"To be" verb identification:
http://www.aztekera.com/tools/tobeverbs.php

Topics:
http://www.mseffie.com/handouts/110personal.html

Recommended Memoirs

Angelou, Maya: *I Know Why the Caged Bird Sings*
Baker, Russell: *Growing Up*
Barrington, Judith: *Lifesaving*
Bartok, Mira: *The Memory Palace*
Bragg, Rick: *All Over but the Shoutin'*
Buchwald, Art: *Too Soon to Say Goodbye*
Chaudhuri, Maria: *Beloved Strangers*
Donoghue, Denis: *Warrenpoint*
Graham, Katharine: *Personal History*
Homes, A.M.: *The Mistress's Daughter*
Karr, Mary: *The Liars' Club*
Kilgour, Mary Cameron: *Me May Mary*
Matthiessen, Peter: *The Snow Leopard*
McCourt, Frank: *Angela's Ashes*
Newman, Leigh: *Still Points North*
Rodgers, Joni: *Bald in the Land of Big Hair*
Santiago, Esmeralda: *When I Was Puerto Rican*
Solnit, Rebecca: *The Faraway Nearby*
Trillin, Calvin: *About Alice*
Walls, Jeannette: *The Glass Castle*
Wolff, Tobias: *In Pharaoh's Army*
Volk, Patricia: *Stuffed: Adventures of a Restaurant Family*

Additional memoirs are listed on my website:
www.susiehbaxter.com

Index

Notes

Notes

Notes

Notes

Notes

Notes

Made in the USA
Monee, IL
19 May 2020